# BIG
# MAN
# SMALL
# EUROPE

# BIG
# MAN
# SMALL
# EUROPE

*poems by* **Tristan Niskanen**

*atmosphere press*

# CONTENTS

## *Part I: A Love Affair with The U.K.*

## Part II: Drinking Songs in Europe

## Part III: Travel Ballads in North Africa & the Middle East

# PART I
## *A Love Affair with The U.K.*

# The Ambassadors on Acid

Where's the punishment for the ambassadors on acid?
There's grandeur in the capital
that opens doors like Canadian Embassy.
Video games & Dior at the V&A
call me Big Man Small Europe today.

The Beatles are at Bedford
after a walk through St. John's Wood
I stroll across Abbey Road before
smoking in a cemetery
by Regent's Park, NW8.

Shoutout Zadie Smith;
peace revelations Mr. Mos;
kingdom sweet bodyguards;
no shakes with no burger;
Soho bumping French House.

The gallery is all the Queen's
but here's Yves' room &
it's all for us.

The ambassadors on acid
spliffing around the park.

# The Thames

The Thames, which I call Timmy
ain't tiny nor too tidy
but it's a mud highway for ships and curious souls.

The two Sphinx on the river look after her &
Cleopatra—
the ship. But the obelisk recalls Egypt of course &
now we remember that Cleopatra too.

Royal Festival Hall & the London Eye evoke British
pride.
Harmony prepares for a midday voyage.
Big Ben stays hidden under construction.
The city is awake today but I only hear the wind.

Although grime water is like hydrated music,
the river shines brighter than the Shard.

We have to microdose the Thames
because we need to build immunity.
The water wars are coming.
No one is safe.
We'll all be thirsty &
only every one if anyone after will pay.

We have to microdose the Thames.
Pump sewage and grime into our veins
& hopefully we can develop salt osmosis.
Where will we drink?
How much time is left?

# London Novels

dark dirty filth criminality
streets spread out sense of spaces
and distinct spaces that contrast threatening
enclosed labyrinth claustrophobic
mythology of london opportunity anonymity
contrast with country between neighborhoods
imperialism thames street naming
center of empire docks suburbs
site of detection mysterious baker street irregulars
unknowability of city
bloomsbury middle parks westminster
technology no private moments
post great war green spaces beautiful
side of sensory overload city visual
imperial west
community lower class but upper
art london poetic london aesthetic
visionary west london
immigrant idealized
outsiders public private
boarding house surveillance
blitz anonymous exhaustion
notting hill portobello road
pub hyperbolic caricature of london
mews heathrow britain and world
class tension juxtaposition
river past and present
east haunted by past
dark government entertainment
real estate development
transforming city scape palimpsest
fantastic dense obsessive and insistent

# Meanwhile

meanwhile
absurd comedy shows
beyoncé's lemonade now on spotify
pitchfork hates kanye coachella
yesterday was earth day
yesterday i saw yesterday's score
i didn't like arsenal's last score
but they gotta score if we gon' make it

woke up in a daze this morning
asterisk on hand, advil down the drain
with some cold coffee
and jazzy tube coltrane

and then merlin shows up
here we go yo
whatcha know about skeff anselm
and anselm too
what is god, god to you?

exercising a compelling charm which inspires
devotion in others
is charisma, is not a car
but drive on with ye olde yells of transportation

it's been a while since i've had a camden hells
but their ipa is better
and there are markets better than camden
but camden town still beats any stock market

bless you
mr alfred

lord bless albert
tennyson eating venison
like steve malkmus

a delicacy of phrase is found in the mabinogion
and so is rhiannon
but not fleetwood mac
both still rock
like the stone where excalibur lived

solution revolution
hippies' dream
solution revolution
hippies dream

# BT Tower

Good morning London!
You'll stay with me for the rest of my life.
I'll always remember your purple information band.
Thank you for Valentines and St. George's
for you, I'll always understand.

I've always wanted to see you
and tonight I will.
BT Tower I'm coming
coming to see if you're real.

I've read the legends and I know the history.
From bombings to racing and even secrecy.
You were the tallest from your start until 1980
if London is the mashed potatoes,
you're my gravy.

I think you must be CCTV HQ
because closed to the public,
what else do you do?
No more restaurant, no more microwave
but fiber optics help our technology behave.

BT Tower look to the sky for me
177 meters, you can be high for me.
As far as my eyes can see
if I was a building, you're what I'd be.

I don't need to fly over the moon.
I only want to fly over you like Harry Potter.
What could be better in London?
Nothing to me sounds smarter

so remember me BT Tower
even when I'm far away
because forever always
I'll think of you every day.

# Tintern Abbey 2019

Upon arrival
Center stones in a river valley
We walk amongst the ruins
Like we're ones too
The birds have the strongest voices in this valley
I think the river is Wye
But I don't know
Why has the universe brought me here today?

I had a picnic with my thoughts
And added a layer of dust to this history
It's this abbey or Abbey Road magical mystery
Spiritual religious or just musical

Switching angles to stay out of shade
To stare at the sun on stone
To sit and just be alone
I wonder if that tree bloomed today

Inside now and the ghosts don't talk
This empty skeleton is full of peaceful breath
These columns still dream of heaven
Why am I celebrating this old ruin?
Maybe I think I'm speaking for myself too

How convenient at the cross
The sun looks me in my eyes
So I sit and wait
Maybe it's time to pray

# Welsh Slate

I feel like Welsh slate
Late great castle building mate
Strata Florida wind is unlike any Florida breeze I've
felt
But they also don't have sheep like they do here

There's a fog upon the heath
And all my friends are in strawberry swing
Singing songs in dungeons
The rocks rock here
And the moss makes them rolling stones
Oh, those sheep
Rolling hills of endless green
Dreaming of a Blue Jay Way

It feels like a medieval year
Tumultuous time of war and fear
Another abbey in ruins
Another world in ruins

Will we make it to the tree?
I think he's buried there

# The Llanberis Pub

Bangers and mash or the cawl
¿Porque no los dos?

A Guinness washes it down nicely
But I'm sure you knew that

What do you do after one of the best days of your life?
I say you try and get another one

So I dream of another one
Either tomorrow or the future

I've got a love that I hope is the future
I believe and it will be as long as you do too

# Hail in Wales

Hail in Wales
On cliffs in Aberystwyth
The shale or slate
Is slick and not thick
Rather thin
Could be the mountain's skin

Sunshine breaks through the clouds
Like God
The light always glows

Dark and stormy
Rain shower drinks
Take a moment
Take a sip this mountain is actually a hill

I've been three months in London
Three days in Wales
During my journey I've discovered
Travel is like hail
It's random, cool, flies from the sky
& makes you ponder water & life

# Morning Dew in Aberystwyth

I woke up with dreams of the love of my life
I stepped outside and the sea said good morning
I waved back and walked out to the castle
Since '98 at since 1277

On the way back
The tide was crashing in
The clouds and water
Were plotting mischief
But I found some coffee and a Cornish pasty

A journey through Wales
Sounds like 20,000 leagues under the sea
But in this yellow submarine
There are no whales to see
Just some castles
And maybe some to be or not to be

Now I'm amongst the fog and sheep in Snowdonia
The landscape is their flag
If only I find the dragon

# Iechyd Da!

On a hole in the wall street,
behind the Caernarfon Castle,
there's a Welsh toast: Iechyd Da!

Inside the beer walls,
we'll take two Lleugwydions
because they seem to be the best and most local brew.

We drink for the future memory
and for this poem.
We also enjoy the hoppy taste
on a rainy day.

These are magical wizard mabinogibeers.
They drink us to a pub where we eat a
fireside Welsh sampler.

Then it's back through the wall,
back past the castle,
a short walk home to Victoria Harbor.

# Ben Twthill

A hike up a lil' hill named Twthill is a thrill
The view rocks on top of some rocks and
pairs nicely with a drink on the rocks.

When it rains like pebble sand,
a cuppa is nice at a caffi.

When there's a castle view
I feel like Eddy One
or maybe Max, the Roman dreaming.

I dream when I'm here
The only thing that's missing is my dear
lovely love of my life.

# Mt. Windon

I'm a flying squirrel
and if that's Mt. Snowdon,
this is Mt. Windon.

I met a lamb at a whispering tree that told me
the Welsh hills have eyes
but not to worry
because they're eyes of friendly dragons,
here in the valley of nature's peace.

Thankfully there's an alcove for a poet
and as weird as it sounds
I feel like making love to this rock.

## Slate and Mead

The force of life
You never know where it'll take you
You just gotta be ready for the opportunities
Because if you're open and positive
The universe will help bring you happiness
I know
Been here before
But also the other side of the game
It feels like the last donut of the night now
And we played "The End" while trying our first mead
Snowdon's honey is sweet like the people here
And how could you not be in Llanberis?
It is a city on the edge of forever
Life is like a Welsh gate
You might know you might not
Either way you'll pass through just fine

# Castell Penglog y Defaid (The Sheep's Skull Castle)

I am no king no prince
But I have a castle
I climb mountains and waterfalls
Because I'm going to our castle
What are those boulders over yonder?
That will be our castle
We explore like archaeologists
Now these stones must be a castle
He finds a sheep skull
This must be Penglog y Defaid
In other words this is
The Sheep Skull's Castle

# St. George's is Shakespeare's Bday

Cittie of Yorke is Sam Smith.
So is all the ye oldes,
so do all the roads in London lead to pubs.

Local pub-mud lad tells us he's six deep and ain't even
pissed yet,
celebrating St. George's like it's his birthday.
He tells us to find Ye Olde Mitre.
Down Chancery Lane, by bishops head and pole,
down the alley, no advertisements.
Cheers lads!

Now underneath the bridge by the Thames,
the lonely violinist plays Harry Potter
with his bow like wand
and his cinematic song.

We're at the Globe for Hank IV
on the birthday of Sir Will.
The sun and St. Paul's bells
cast spells on my mind as I pass time drinking hells.

We're groundlings today.
Wizard professor punt asked us out for a pint.
He says go Hotspurs, but Hotspur dies
imitating the cries of the sun.

The open air Globe makes me want to say:
"Give me a cup of sack and quit horsing around"
like Falstaff. I wonder if I might be wondered at.

Low tide lets rocks skip over the Thames under
moonlight.
Dancing dreams on cityscapes, looking for the escape,
This is life.

Blackfriars to home,
the myth of the Holborn Circus.
No beer here in the City of London.
Greene King comparisons lead to root beer at the party
store.

## Tottenham Court Road
## is always moving

With the help of my friends,
this what God feel like.
To be lucy at the rising sun drinking diamonds.

The falafel man runs an impressive small business
out of a telephone booth—
like Cal's phone repair man.

Tottenham Court Road is always moving
like the weary bearded Coloradan traveler
who likes to say there is a house in New Orleans.

# Professor

Society is the enemy
Theater is a way for a city to talk about itself
The one thing you should get from this class
Switch to decaf
Play like Antigone
People can fall prey to unpleasant narratives
Always a bit of politics in all of it
Yay!
It's a proper pipe like Watson
Let me tell you about the ancient greeks
Where the hell was I going with that?
Theater always takes on fate
I brought the tie because I like to play with it
professionally
Let's just move forward
Next I'll be ranting here to thin air
You'll be thinking who was that guy with a cardigan
Fate!
As a Marxist
Fate!
It must be like an epic painting
Fate!
Karl Marx's grave
Fate!
Active spectator
Offers a theater that changes the world
Brecht is unapologetic about it
Mother courage
Fate!

# Battle Abbey to Sissinghurst

There's no anti-climb paint innit
There's no sparrow hawk in the sky
On a class trip reading idylls
Trying like wine to make summer in my veins

Tower Hill station intrigues
And electrolyting gherkins look
Cool amongst Tower Hamlets

I dream of Brocéliande
Wishing in the age of love
Like innervisions in my mind
Laid back, sittin' here feelin' dizzee

Innocent is naked juice
Broken banana juice
Song lyric is:
"The present is a gift and I just want to be"

Tears fall by vibrant yellow fields
I am going to be

Domino Delorean dreams of summerset marshes
Who are the Normans?
Upon the heath
They won here
The battle of Hastings created a geo-shift that goes on
Until Brexit shenanigans
Not ill prepared, ill-advised and sick

Did earls wear sweatshirts here?
The ponds and swamp make me hallucinate Shrek
The purple bells and oak soldiers
Form like an army
I wish we could larp
And hold the line like Hodor

# The Great Red and White

Every Vodafone employee is an Arsenal fan
The great red and white
Every flower is blooming in the park
More great red and white
And green and blue are so classic
So classic days be some of the best

Tai Chi in Russell Square
With tomatoes challenging gravity
Sir Bedford's statue follows us around
Protecting us and taking our bird shit

Writing this poem feels like déjà vu
Or cosmic consciousness
Something to that effect
Perhaps it was written
On another classic
Illmatic day
Just like Nas is like
Freedom of

# Notre Dame is burning

The professor and student share a pint
at Lord John Russell after class
to discuss fate, immigration & literature.

A warm haze has enclosed the city for today
but Russell Square is still a shrine of spring.
Notre Dame is burning.

The newspapers are on fire &
More newspapers look on fire than rolling papers
today
Don't you love the pub culture?
It's more relaxed than club culture and more fun
anyway

# St. Bart's

Jesus is a little wooden statue or a golden painting
The whispers of the ghosts play Bach today
It's the Wednesday before Easter
Sunny morning
And I've made my way to St. Bart's
I'm here for class
But I'll write poetry
I'll find time for meditation
And for wooden Jesus
I'll pray

# The George

At the George Pub and I feel like
Austerlitz could be sitting across from me
Or Samuel Johnson working on a dictionary
I'm working on something bitter
A poem about
Life's current beer for me
Yes, life can be bitter
But it can be butter
And have glitter
And although it feels like litter
We can live with trash
But not in the river

# Lamb and Flag

The first poet laureate of England almost was done to death
In the alley where we walk
Some rogues almost got Dryden
But they didn't
And they didn't get me
Because rogue is written on my shoes
We drank some brews at the Lamb and Flag
Because we've got to risk
Can life be a blessing
Or worth possessing
Like Troilus and Cressida

# Arthur is not dead

Arthur is not dead
Here in this world he changed his life
And so God save the king
He lives in Cuba with Pac
Listening to .Paak
Sangre or sangreal?
There as a man's heart is set
Bloody holy grail
Spamalot tastes better than spam
And TV show Arthur
Just as good as dragon tales
Drinking Merlin magic ales
That must be a butterbeer

# Extinction Rebellion

I've stumbled upon a couple protests in a couple days
The protesters in Paris wore yellow
Police do here in London
All funny hats

Extinction rebellion
How are we supposed to fight?
On the water thinking of the water wars
They're coming, propaganda tells us
Humans rebel for life
The government has failed you

Like always it's hard to feel global warming
When it's cold outside
At least they have sunshine for the march
Trees as flags
Act now
Wave your leafs

Drink water while you can
The Thames ain't safe
And we ain't either

# Part II
## *Drinking Songs in Europe*

# Rolling like the hills outside Madrid

Years memories I have thought future dreams now
reality
What it means to finally be in Spain
Vain but I feel it in my veins
Rolling like the hills outside Madrid

Late fictions supreme religions all feelings
Of no feeling only dreaming and repeating life
As if it comes at me like Don Quixote
Or circular friends in a park or palm
Trees or the breeze or the sweet green
Grass that makes time pass faster than the speed of the
clouds

Words as lame as shoes'll do for arts only when it's the
middle of the night
I always need a drum kick
Build the bass like a drunken poet
With citrus and horns
The key to life
Happy music for days and extra days

# A stream in Granada

Steams of, stream nearby
Stream of consciousness
Walk on by

No duck duck
Only two goose goose
The sun is high
The sun is loose

Bridge over stream
12 string never scream
Aquamarine water
A stream of a dream

I just want pineapple juice
And a big book to read
Under the shade tree by the stream

I just want to build sand castles
And find old pottery by the stream
By the stream, I want to make friends with dogs
And tell my friends about the dogs I met by the stream

By the way I'm writing this in the stream
And feel like always our lives are streams

# Un sueño de Toledo

In the park by the Moorish walls
I have un sueño de Toledo

In it I swim in el río Tagus
I paint pictures of el puente de Alcántara
My bed is in el Cristo de la Cruz
And here I have a sword

I have un sueño de Toledo
And it's my life here right now

Yellow sunshine yellow buildings
My love in a yellow dress
Hello sunshine give me a sueño
And then I'll enjoy my rest

# El Salvador en Sevilla

Falling religion but always ascending
Glittered gold vaults gilded
Is it to cover up faults and guilt?
El Salvador en Sevilla
A church wondering at the heavens

I wonder what would religion be without symbolism?
Praise poetry is praying poetry
I feel at peace in all places of worship
Yet shalt not worship blindly
I don't see exactly clearly
So I question
Is El Salvador the divine savior or Sevilla?
Or is it just El Salvador en Sevilla?

# La madrugada en Granada

Feeling like frijoles frescos in la madrugada en
Granada
A siesta is the puente to the fuente
At the top of the hill at the end of the day
In Sacromonte

In Sacromonte
The church views the Alhambra
Songs are in the streets
The moon is in the blue sky
Tears in my eyes
Y tú también
Díos ríos
Cat's eye in cacti

# El Retiro

I have visions of El Escorial en el Prado
Ahora estoy en el Retiro
With thoughts of the preservation of art

There's more than one Mona Lisa
How many times have we thought about religion?
Because it's even painted with aventurine

I want light and lift like El Greco
Some memories of Granada
And answers to what Flemish is

I don't have a store of madness
And I'm not the portrait of a humanist
Yet I'm framed and floating
Like an open triptych

# The Gardens of Atocha

Nature take us over
Like the foliage by trains' gates
In the heart of Madrid

Grow green grow strong grow big
Give us a taste of life
In the center of transportation

The gardens of Atocha
Keep my spirits up like mocha
I live amongst the flowers here
Because I'm one and so are you

Stay alive gardens of Atocha
In this world of confusion
You're one of the few things that give us hope

# El Alcázar

En el Alcázar, I enjoy the arabic art
More specifically Almohad architecture
A palm palace
El palacio de Pedro
Psychedelic patterns
Repetition and perfection in geometry
Design is king with this royalty

I touch tiles and feel smiles
Seville ceramics serenade me
But I do glimpse horrors of history

While savoring sour oranges
And imagining I'm in Dorne
I look out over the garden
And I see more lushness than the Garden of Eden
So I think Alcázar
Is more sweet than any azúcar

# April in Amsterdam

Tranquil colors look psychedelic even without drugs
The bikes of Amsterdam swarm and sing like bees
Some things sting and trees flow everywhere
Like the canal water
And the two-euro water
Sometimes the choice's beer

I love Amsterdam for its nature and stroop
The drugs are mixed
And red lights make me uncomfortable
Green light to the green
Dock says 420
Don't really need anything else
But coffee always helps
And even 2019 Vondel park
Looks like the sixties

## The Flying Pig

Peer pressure can put you down crazy roads
You don't know where you'll end up
But how else do you be recklessly young
Not dumb and travel the world?

Everyone needs to see pigs fly
At least for a night
With a roomful of bongs & heartburn pizza
At least it's cheap
And world company
Hot air balloons for the ride home

We didn't come to Amsterdam
For the Heineken & weed
We have that back home

We didn't come to Amsterdam
For the tulips & windmills
I've been to Holland, Michigan

We came to see pigs fly
At a hostel with the homies
& to serenade ourselves with Jacques Brel

# Budapest

If you sleep on the couch
You swim in the Buda's bath
After climbing a mountain
Maybe running
Maybe risking your life

If you sleep on the couch
And use a Buddha pillow
You drink a beer at the top of that mountain
And feel like the queen of the Danube

If you climb on sticks
And jump on trampolines
Climbing under bridges becomes second nature
The best part of Pest is when
The city mixes with nature

# Szimpla Kert

Run into a ruin bar
And feel like you're on rum and a bar
You're not too far from your place
So don't worry if you don't remember her face

Her story is she's friends with Bill Murray
She's on a bachelorette party
But our hookah's more inviting
Where's the bride?

We are the united nations
Here at Szimpla Kert
Budapest sounds better than Ludacris
It's beautiful & nothing hurts

After dick bread and graffiti guest books
Pictures of friends helps remember
So does returning to the same place
The next night

# The river stick man

The river stick man walks on walks on
He wears a blue coat
With two bottles on two bottles on
Ready for a scooter or ready for a ride
The oldest amusement park has a swing ride
Psychedelic characters and a dive bar
It's cinematic like Hawke and Delpy

The river stick man will eat schnitzel
And might smoke a rello on the roof
On the nights he sleeps in the treehouse
Vienna is the second city
Not Chicago, just the second destination

He has his first coney island before castles and Klimt
His nights are at the vinyl bar
Where he might hear 50 Cent
He tries gelato and plays Billy Joel
At least he represents

# Kafkaesque Czech

No pills, just pilsners.
Urquell or Staropramen.
It's Praha not Prague
but I still say Prague.

The bars have speakeasy edibles.
The THC sets you free
but don't get lost amongst the cobblestones & bridges
because you might get eaten by a gargoyle
or swept away by Vltava.

Stain glass & old stone
red roofs & spiral staircases.
All evoke freedom like Lennon's wall
but we hope it don't all fall to something like Lenin.

The public gets redone so it's in Czech.
Is it?
I don't know but I had a good time
although it was all so Kafkaesque.

# The Big Lil' Island of Malta

A sprawling maze like ant hill
but more like a sandstone castle.
How many buses must you take
To get from St. Juilian's to the Blue Grotto?

As many as it takes
because the color of the water is enough to satisfy.
Blue in as many colors as you think
when you have Meditteranean dreams.

Right down the street is some of our oldest history
3,600 BC at Hagar Qim.
A 'temple' more wondrous than Stonehenge,
second only to Gobekli Tepe.

Lizards love to lounge & so do I.
We all know the sister-site Mnajdna is better
because it looks like a fun fort that any kid
throughout humanity would love to play in.

More travels on the bus got me
feeling like I'm going to Ba Sing Se.
Statues at these megalithic temples look like Uncle Iroh
& we know anywhere goes better with a cup of tea.

Golden blue golden sunset skies,
cardoons & carob trees,
all have me enjoying the summer breeze,
& feeling free like bees in Maltese purple flowers.

## May to May

I been around the world
Today in Malta
Last year in Hong Kong
And yesterday in Jordan

The past few days for me
Have been Red, Dead, Mediterranean Sea
The world will always be a vast mystery
But from May to May I've learned so much history

From May to May I've lived across the world
New York to near Yorkshire
But Colorado will always be home
Hol' up, mountains will always be home

I've grown
Maybe only an inch in height
But otherwise wiser than most my younger nights
I've seen places of knights
And so much royalty
I've learned lessons of loyalty
But still don't understand tin foil

From May to May
I've been May to December
Mos Def
I'll be in Venice before December
The Italian job for me
And Mos Def

My toes have touched two more continents
I'm content

And had many revelations with ten
Learning Zen
And what it means to be one with zero

I still feel like zero
Shia and shy
Digging holes
Constantly filling holes
And re-reading books with trolls
And dreaming of finding the next Dead Sea Scrolls

I've been everywhere
Like a cheesy enterprise
I guess my new dream
Is to eat cheese on the Star Trek Enterprise
This morning I opened my eyes
And felt like I was in Tatooine

# A Night at the Champion's League

This year the Gunners didn't make it
But two UK teams did
So what should the kid do?

Tottenham's not hot
Sugar cane over Harry Kane
The only Spur I support is Son

Since it ain't red and white
The Reds better win tonight
Plus my friends wants to be
Forever LFC

In Malta watching football
I'm just a boy in da corner kick
Watching Salah kick
And my friends are sippin' Cisk

It's the big screen in St. George's Bay
And it's the 6th time
The title's gone the Reds' way

On the next day with a cuppa tea
Thinking about my life
The mystery and opportunity
Oh yes, it's lucky me

# Randacropolis

In this heat, in this economy?
On Jesus, on Athena, on Dionysos
Slippery stone, the art of Artemis
Honey made, green birds, rooftop daft punk
Are the ancient Greeks and Greek gods still with us
today?

Rooftop to rooftop
Sunrise to sunset
Three days in Athens
The world is not enough

Where's the baklava?
Where's the honey ice cream?
Where's the Greek yogurt?

I've been at peace in this place far from Nice
The water's closer than I thought
& the mountains remind me of home

I see how this place makes a good home
Mind, body, spirit lives through
the soul & you can feel it on a cobblestone stroll

The park is Artemis' gift
Just like the other gods inspire
I want to run the Olympic track
Just like how I had to taste ouzo

Is a movie at Cine Paris the same as the theater of
Dionysus?

I think so since you can see the Acropolis & imagine yourself
as a lucky old Greek who got to see Aeschylus &
Sophocles

I need to read up on my Socrates
And the Iliad & Odyssey are still on my bookshelf

I did push ups where Aristotle did his thang
& I'm doing mine right here
Can't help but eat olives
And I love the coffee

Athens is quite like you think it is
These places of rich history have a habit of being like
that
I'm happy to be here
& this one's for you, all that couldn't be here

# Keri Beach 6:06 pm


A Mediterranean diet
I mean liveit
Could be just the sea
The water
Just one color
Blue giving life
I feel like the fish
Eating olives
And I can never get enough honey
I'm a turtle swimming freely
Looking at the mountains
And starfish
The moon is already up
But there are still many hours to the day

# Paris

Alcoholic waters coursing through the city
as though the Eiffel was an olive colored artery that
pumps wine.
They say they love the vine & who could not?
I still see Dionysus in the sky past these history books.

What is Paris but everyone's collective dream?
Your movie, my song,
your novel, my painting.
The art & the heart and more
Paris forever
the art & the heart and more.

There's a scooter in the river,
dime bag on sand,
cigarettes everywhere,
on ground & open hand.

The trees breathe
as water glitters.
Hey! I just found a lucky penny.

Another scooter in the river
& broken glass shattered, glimmering like the river.

Underneath the Passerelle Léopold-Sédar-Senghor
There's a stairway to the other side.
Oh sun, how I love to kiss you today.
You guide me on my journey,
a wanderer in the magic city
Where shall I find myself?
Wherever you might be.

# The Seine

Drinking games on the Seine all the same
Still I want to join
All alone I want to join
But I sing my song
And write these words
I read those words
And I'm not alone
On the Seine
I got good company
With drinking games
All the same
Still I want to join

A café underneath the bridge always satisfies
And there's no cream
Just the americano on the Seine
By Pont Louis-Philippe
Watching birds and Bird and Lime
Just this summer
Worldwide takeover
Like pigeon park worlds
Broken bottles and twisted glasses
Rollerblading stroller mama don't care
She's off to the park
And so should we

## I've always dreamed of being an existentialist

I've always dreamed of being an existentialist
And now I'm here in Paris
How do I feel my essence?
Does it precede existence?

I left my turtleneck in a nicotine dream
My pen lost its ink in my coffee
I wish I could write with Jean, Albert & Simone
But I'm all alone at this café

I'm nauseous so I guess existentialism's okay

## Shakespeare & Co

God bless you Sylvia Beach
for Shakespeare & Co.
From Gertrude to Fitz,
I found Billy and Jack
where you published Ulysses.

Now I try to publish my own.
Thank you for your service,
this bookshop is the perfect discovery
for the strawberry eating & Bordeaux drinking
Seine walker & poetry writer

Who writes only for you
Who writes only for me

# Virgil

Virgil's even got the water on lock
But I'm not naive enough to buy Evian

Foundation is right up around the corner
Off white skies today

I saw YSL yesterday in Paris
Dior designed my dreams in London

Paris is his city
What am I wearing today?

A new blue sweater
Because it's needed when the weather's grey

# Falstaff Café

The blind man stares at me
after every bite of his calzone
but it's okay because I return the glance
& sip my French wine just fine

I'm out of food at Falstaff café
I wonder about Shakespeare allusions
& know that most things in life
Are just illusions

or some consequence of
dreams & destiny or
an ill society I'd like
to cure but don't know how

Maybe with poetry
Maybe with poetry

## We live! We die!

I liked my waiter last night
He wasn't too superfluous
He poured the Beaujolais smoothly
Smiled & walked away

As I stepped out at Saint-Germain-des-Prés
I discovered Les Deux Magots
Home of the existentialists
The stranger from Colorado arrived

I must write
Because now
We're at Café de Flore
Another existentialist den

Oh Paris I love you
And I must write
We live!
I must write
We die!

# Part III
## *Travel Ballads in North Africa & the Middle East*

# Egyptian Sun

In the Egyptian sun at last
I just wanna scream RA!

I don't know how long I can last
In this heat & can't eat like a fast

Broken with a Lebanese feast
Skin tan no longer like bleach

Pool side cooling
Room air condition cooling

Ruling my bucket list like a pharaoh
Nile dreaming always

Another day in Egypt
Another dreamer

Underneath blazing summer sun
It's Ramadan

And I'm gon see
The pyramids tomorrow

# Sunset at the Red Sea

Sunset at the Red Sea
Let the kids run on the beach
Like they're supposed to
Let them be free
Throw rocks
And laugh
Like they're supposed to
When the sun sets behind the mountains
It's time to jump in the sea
When you can't swim
Just wade in
Let summer begin
And then
Let yourself dream
Like you're supposed to

# Morocco is Colorado

Morocco is Colorado
Colored and clay
Like a tajin baking all day
The city of red
Is full of cats and cobras
Covered markets
And no Corollas
So many bikes so many bikes
It's the opposite of a city of lights
The city at night
Feasts until the sun come up
Because when it rises
The fasts begin
It's Ramadan
Which makes me think upon
My life, myself, and God

# Rooftop in Marrakech

I dream of hash
When I'm in high places
When I see the dancing moonlight
I think of movies in Miami

I think of elevators of 305
And songs of 3005
Something Childish
But something cool

Something like me
Something like you

On this rooftop in Marrakech
I drink mint tea
I write these poems
I think of the Berbers

When I see the Atlas Mountains
Way past the medina
I think of the Rockies

# Ramadan

Fahrenheit 115 don't make sense
Neither does 46 C
Sounds like a bad airplane seat
And this heat
Makes feet melt like molten lava
Feels like volcanoes bursting
Can't believe people working
During Ramadan

Ramadan Sobhi is a winger
And he reps the club of the century
In the city of centuries
That looks like our dystopian future's outcast
Al Ahly's games never on Comcast
Ain't on demand
But it has more demand than most
Being the most decorated footballers in Africa

In Africa I feel like I've returned
Even though not the same for me
And never been here before
This land of early civilization
Has a calling for me
I hear the pyramids ring in my ears
Like the cell phone the sphinx never had

Had I done more research
I would've known how many people live in Cairo
More than double NYC
And more haze than Jimi could breathe
No breeze
Just ancient looking moons and suns

And the Sun Ra over head
Like the jazz in my headphones
Praying to God
That I never forget Egypt

# A lil' vill named Imlil

Far from the sounds and souls of Marrakech
In a lil' vill named Imlil
Hassan leads us up a hill
To a beautiful waterfall

At last, lost in the Atlas
Lost city, last city
Perhaps this is Atlantis

The vantage of the peaks
Is pure majestic and marvelous mystique

Are you an Argonaut for argan?
Or are you planting seeds in the soil for olive oil?

Is your body for profit?
Or is it a prophet?
Like a body Bodhisattva

Mint tea in the rug room
Mint tea at Hassan's
Thinking life's a religion
These mountains are imams

# Welcome to Jordan

Made a friend named Karim in Marrakech
Ramadan mubarak
From Morocco to Egypt celebrated al-fitr
Rooftop Ramadan Kareem
Egypt no Mubarak

Sunset break fast to feast
You don't sleep as well in the east
You rest best in the west
That's only after death
Or the sun's last breath

Today I breathe in the bay
Or should I say gulf
My head is in the Red
It's Aqaba
Welcome to Jordan

# Peace & Panic

Bumping DAMN. on the beach
Hot damn, it's hot
& I need some water
Like Kendrick
Holy music & holy water
The soundtrack to my life
With harmonies from the Red Sea

As sunset approaches
I run through prayer & meditation
Urges to do yoga & smoke
Thoughts of the day
Of swimming & shawarma
Thinking of palaces & Petra
Wondering what it all is & who we all are

The world around me is so beautiful
Yet we are all in a storm
Both quite literally
& more than metaphorically
There's a balance everywhere
Like it feels swimming in the great unknown
Peace & panic

We all must be astronauts
But none have even seen our whole earth
There's so much out there
Waiting
& we wait
Life is always changing
Because it's how it is

# Mud Face

Two scoops should be sufficient
You'll float anyway
Sands'll do
But this ain't Zanzibar
So why don't you
Dig in the mud

Sally silly capitalism sells
The same sediment for 3 JDs
You can get it for free
If you find the right friends

Mud face at the Dead Sea
Is the key
To helping you not age endlessly
Everybody knows that
But that shouldn't stop you
From enjoying the dead deep blue

# Baptism Site of Jesus Christ

Jesus didn't play basketball
But he was dunked in the Jordan
River like a Chicago Bull

Jesus wasn't baptized at birth
But he swam in the light
With his cuzzo John

The baptism site of Jesus Christ
Is but a puddle today
Near the muddy banks of today's river

The area splits Israel and Jordan
Sounds like a middle east
And there's churches here for all

# Petra

Deep in the desert
Deep in the canyon
Down in the dirt
There you have Petra

The forgotten city
The cave dwelling
Star Wars feeling
Jordanian oasis

In Petra the camels and horses
And people and flies
Mingle together
Just like it's the 5th century BC

The place feels mythical
And magical and might be
The symmetry and subtly
Is as efficient as it's effective
The city's still reflective of us

Always building
Always visiting
Keeping up our fascination
With our past selves and us

# ABOUT ATMOSPHERE PRESS

Atmosphere Press is an independent, full-service publisher for excellent books in all genres and for all audiences. Learn more about what we do at atmospherepress.com.

We encourage you to check out some of Atmosphere's latest releases, which are available at Amazon.com and via order from your local bookstore:

*A Dream of Wide Water,* poetry by Sharon Whitehill

*Radical Dances of the Ferocious Kind*, poetry by Tina Tru

*The Woods Hold Us,* poetry by Makani Speier-Brito

*My Cemetery Friends: A Garden of Encounters at Mount Saint Mary in Queens, New York*, nonfiction and poetry by Vincent J. Tomeo

*Report from the Sea of Moisture,* poetry by Stuart Jay Silverman

*The Enemy of Everything*, poetry by Michael Jones

*The Stargazers,* poetry by James McKee

*The Pretend Life*, poetry by Michelle Brooks

*Minnesota and Other Poems*, poetry by Daniel N. Nelson

# ABOUT THE AUTHOR

Tristan Niskanen likes to think of himself as a creator. It might be a poem, it might be a song, it might just be an idea. He spends as much time as possible outdoors, chasing sunsets. When he's not outside fishing or hiking, he's usually working on some project. He hails from the mountains of Colorado and recently graduated from Colgate University.